FLUTE
REPERTOIRE

HIROSE
[New Edition]
Blue Train / Marine City / Papillon
for Flute Orchestra

Revised by Akira Aoki, Hiroshi Hari, Yukako Yamagami

廣瀬量平
［新版］
フルート・オーケストラのための
ブルー・トレイン／マリン・シティ／パピヨン

青木明・播博・山上友佳子 校訂

音楽之友社

ONGAKU NO TOMO EDITION

まえがき

今回、音楽之友社から《ブルー・トレイン》《マリン・シティ》《パピヨン》の廣瀬量平フルート・オーケストラ三部作の楽譜が出版されたことは、フルート界にとっては一大快挙である。

日本フルート協会創立50周年記念パーティーで、音楽之友社から「邦人作曲家のフルート作品を継続して出版したい。廣瀬量平はどうでしょうか」との提案があり、すぐにOKの返事を出した。

フルートファンだけでなく、一般の方も、スコアと映像を見ながら、あの独特の廣瀬量平サウンドはどういう楽譜から生まれ出てくるのだろう、とチェックする楽しみ方もある。

この機会に、ぜひ体験していただきたい。

播 博
武蔵野音楽大学名誉教授

Foreword

The publication by Ongaku no Tomo Sha of three works for flute orchestra by Ryōhei Hirose, *Blue Train*, *Marine City* and *Papillon* is an event of major importance for the flute world.

At a party held to mark the fiftieth anniversary of the Japan Flutists Association, a representative of Ongaku no Tomo Sha mentioned that the publishing company would like to continue issuing works for flute by Japanese composers and suggested the name of Ryōhei Hirose. The Association gave its immediate assent to this proposal.

Devotees of the flute along with music-lovers in general will now have the opportunity to peruse the scores of Ryōhei Hirose's work and enjoy the experience of seeing how the distinctive sound of this composer's work comes about.

Hiroshi Hari
Professor Emeritus, Musashino Academia Musicae

目　次

まえがき（播 博）……………… 2
Foreword（Hiroshi Hari）

作品について（廣瀬周平）………… 4
About works（Shūhei Hirose）

演奏の手引き（青木 明）………… 6
A guide to performance（Akira Aoki）

ブルー・トレイン …… 8
Blue Train

マリン・シティ ……… 19
Marine City

パピヨン ………………… 23
Papillon

パート譜はダウンロード購入いただけます。
詳細は音楽之友社商品ページをご覧ください。
https://www.ongakunotomo.co.jp/catalog/detail.php?code=609044

ブルー・トレイン	作曲	1979年
	初演	1979年9月20日　上野学園 石橋メモリアルホール
		東京フルートアンサンブル・アカデミー
		指揮：青木 明
マリン・シティ	作曲	1980年
	初演	1980年1月12日　東京文化会館 大ホール
		日本フルートフェスティヴァル100人のフルーティスト
		指揮：森 正
パピヨン	作曲	1980年
	初演	1980年7月9日　上野学園 石橋メモリアルホール
		東京フルートアンサンブル・アカデミー
		指揮：青木 明

作品について

廣瀬周平

ブルー・トレイン

　廣瀬量平にとってフルート・オーケストラ作品の1作目にあたり、東京フルートアンサンブル・アカデミーにとっても委嘱1作目になります。初演では2度のアンコールを呼ぶセンセーショナルな成功を収め、いまや世界中で演奏される、現代の古典曲となっています。現実音がはっきりと音楽の中で描写され、汽笛、連結器のきしみ、車窓を飛び去る踏切音とそのドップラー効果、レールの継ぎ目を越えるガタンゴトンという音が、シンプルな三和音の4/4で刻まれつつ走ります。

　ブルー・トレインとは、ご存じの通り夜行列車のこと。「常に進行している規則的なリズム、それにブルー、つまりメランコリーと夢、ファンタジーをフルートの澄んだハーモニーに託してみようと思った」とは、廣瀬の初演時の言葉です。この曲はいろいろな領域に影響を及ぼし、NHKではこの曲をもとに映像詩が制作放送され、尺八合奏（三橋貴風編曲）、リコーダー合奏（吉澤 実編曲）、クラリネット八重奏（編曲者不詳）にもなっています。

マリン・シティ

　第2回日本フルートフェスティヴァルのために日本フルート協会から委嘱され、森 正の指揮で100人のフルーティストによって初演されました。フルート・オーケストラ作品としては2作目です。マリン・シティとは海底都市のイメージであり、ジュール・ヴェルヌの小説「海底二万マイル」も構想のヒントになっているようです。水中の遠景に、かすかに見えてくる海底都市というような、見えない映像を音で見せる描写は作曲者の得意とするところ。水中の重たげな頼りなさ、薄暗い視界の不確かさや光の揺れなどの表現は、フルート・オーケストラという編成を得てこその描写であり、圧倒される音響を生んでいます。

　この楽譜冒頭には「ビブラート厳禁!!」と珍しい指示があります。初演の際の手書き楽譜では、それは日本語で大きく書かれた指示でした。このことは、作曲者がこの曲全体についてイメージする、精密な描写への意欲の表れなのでしょう。

パピヨン

　フルート・オーケストラでは3作目にあたります。作曲者は初演にあたってこう語ります。「今回の新作は《パピヨン》、つまり蝶と名づけた。卵から幼虫になり、やがてさなぎになり、さらに脱皮して蝶になるのを見て、我々の祖先たちは、人間もさまざまな節目を通り、やがて蝶のように天を舞い上がっていくものと考えたようだ。つまり蝶は霊でもあり、また生命の循環、輪廻転生の証しでもあった。さまざまな文様に取り入れられ、また今日でも蝶に狂い蝶を求めて異境をさまよう人は多い。また群れを成して飛翔し、大洋を渡る蝶の姿も感動的である。そんなことをとりとめなく考えながらこの曲に蝶の名をつけた」。

　霊的でもあり、ひらひらゆらゆらと舞い、大群にもなる蝶は、まさにフルート・オーケストラの特徴そのままであると、廣瀬はいろいろな場面で語っています。

About works

Shūhei Hirose

Blue Train

Blue Train was the first work for flute orchestra by Ryōhei Hirose and was composed to a commission from the Tokyo Flute Ensemble Academy. It proved to be a sensational success on the occasion of its première. It has since become a modern classic of its type on an international level. Extra-musical sounds associated with trains and railways are incorporated into the music, including the sound of a train's whistle, the squealing of railway carriage couplers, the sound of the warning bell at the gate of a level crossing and the Doppler effect experienced through a carriage window as the train whizzes past, and the rattle of the rail joint sounds. Such realistic depiction is presented within a simple triadic format in 4/4 time.

'Blue train' is the term used in Japan to refer to night trains. In the programme notes written by the composer on the occasion of the work's first performance, Hirose wrote that 'My idea has been to make use of constantly developing regular rhythms in combination with "blue" melancholy, dreams and fantasy and to entrust the expression thereof to the limpid harmony of a flute ensemble.' The work has had an extensive influence in many quarters: a lyrical video was produced and broadcast by the NHK on the basis of the work, and it has subsequently been arranged for shakuhachi ensemble by Kifū Mitsuhashi, for recorder ensemble by Minoru Yoshizawa, and for clarinet octet.

Marine City

This work was commissioned by the Japan Flutists Association for the 2nd Japan Flute Festival and was first performed by an orchestra of a hundred flautists conducted by Tadashi Mori. This was Hirose's second work for flute orchestra. The image of a marine city was suggested by Jules Verne's novel *Twenty Thousand Leagues Under the Sea*. Hirose excels in the depiction in sound of obscure images, in this case the image of a marine city faintly visible from far away. The representation of the weighty unpredictability of the ocean, of the uncertainty of the gloomy field of vision, and of the fluctuations of light is well suited to the medium of the flute orchestra, which creates an overwhelming soundscape.

The unusual indication 'Not to do VIBRATO!!' appears at the head of the score and was written emphatically in large characters in the manuscript employed for the first performance. It indicates the composer's concern with the intricate portrayal in sound of the image that he envisages as permeating the work as a whole.

Papillon

Papillon is Hirose's third work for flute orchestra. The programme notes written by Hirose on the occasion of the work's première contained the following passage: 'My new work *Papillon* is based on the idea of butterflies (papillons in French) emerging from the egg to become larvae, then turning into a chrysalis, after which they emerge as fully formed butterflies. This idea put me in mind of our own ancestors, who passed through various stages of development to eventually dance up into the heavens just like a butterfly. The butterfly is thus the symbol of the soul and proof of the recurrence of life and metempsychosis. There are many people today who aspire to the ideal of the butterfly, which is incorporated into many designs as a representation of the aspiration to venture into another realm. The sight of a swarm of butterflies in flight across the seas is enormously moving. This is the image I had in mind when I composed this piece and is why I named it *Papillon*.'

On many occasions Hirose has alluded to the way in which a swarm of butterflies, with their spiritual image, fluttering through the skies is the perfect analogy for the features of the flute orchestra.

演奏の手引き

青木 明

ブルー・トレイン

　東京フルートアンサンブル・アカデミーの委嘱で、廣瀬量平氏がフルート・オーケストラを手掛けた最初の作品であり、演奏形態を認知された曲でもあります。今では世界各国でたびたび演奏されています。初演時の2回のアンコールは、フルート・オーケストラの将来を暗示するかのごとく、とても印象的な出来事でした。

　演奏に際しては、全体を構成する三つの基本テンポのうち、2ndフルートがつくる夜行列車の淡いノスタルジーを感じさせるTempoⅠの設定がとても重要です。今回出版される3曲とも2ndフルートがキーポイントですが、寸分違わずタテ線をそろえること、各ソロパートが自由に歌える箇所をつくることが大切です。そこで、2ndフルートの最初の8分音符の刻みは、ただそろえるだけなら1拍目の裏から、イメージを膨らませてスタートする場合は1拍目の頭からのほうがよいと思います。

　2本のピッコロによる汽笛の長さのイメージは、始まりと終わりとでは違うと思いますが、そろって消えるように終えるのは至難の業です。

　TempoⅢの速い6/8でのリズムの乱れは厳禁です。迷わず突っ走ること。また終盤の室内楽風のところは、各パートとも思いっきり歌うことです。

　オプションのコントラバスフルートのほか、ダブルコントラバスフルートの参加も妨げるものではありませんが、過度な低音の増強にならぬよう、ごく適度に低音を添えるような演奏が、この作品らしいと思います。このことは以下2曲でも言えることだと思います。

マリン・シティ

　深い海底都市、空想の世界、神秘、静寂、フルート・オーケストラでこんな表現が出来るのだろうか……。初演時は、元譜（原譜ではない）の8小節目からスタートしました。私はそのカット版（本楽譜）がよいと思います。また、後半 C からの1stフルート一連のSolo（3箇所）は初演時、廣瀬量平氏が冒頭の7小節をカットした後に、指揮台の上で（私の目の前で）書き加えられました。その経緯からも、冒頭の7小節のカットには意味があると思っています。

　初演時にかなりの変更があって、棒の振り方もそれに沿って変更したと記憶しています。

パピヨン

　2ndフルートは秋のうら寂しさに一脈通じるテンポをつくり、1stフルートはそれに乗って歌う。自然界の神秘、静寂、転じて動的な展開はクラスターのやり方次第で決まります。作曲者の指示を忠実に守ることが鍵で、秋の風が寂しく残る蝶の舞です。

A guide to performance

Akira Aoki

Blue Train

Blue Train was the first work for flute orchestra by Ryōhei Hirose and was composed to a commission from the Tokyo Flute Ensemble Academy. It was the work that for the first time generated a general awareness of the flute orchestra as a medium. It is frequently performed today both inside and outside Japan. It was encored twice at its première, its sensational success on that occasion presaging the future of the flute orchestra.

There are three basic tempi employed in the work as a whole. It is very important to set Tempo I, with its mood of pale nostalgia for the night train generated by the second flutes. The second flutes play a key role in all three works in this publication. Precise vertical coordination and creating the framework for the solo parts to sing out freely are essential. The initial quavers (eighth-notes) at the start of the second flute part should be conceived from the half-beat if the aim is merely to achieve coordination or from the first beat if starting with an image in mind.

How the length of the train whistle entrusted to the two piccolos is conceived is likely to differ at the start and at the end, but it's extremely difficult to fade out entirely together.

There should be no irregularity in Tempo III (6/8). It's important to push forward regardless. A very lyrical approach needs to be taken in each of the parts to the chamber music-like writing at the end of the piece.

The double contrabass flute may also be included in the ensemble if the optional contrabass flute is employed, but the nature of this piece and the other two pieces in this set is such that overloading the bottom register of the ensemble would be inappropriate.

Marine City

A city deep in the ocean, a world of fantasy, mystery and tranquillity: is this something that a flute orchestra is capable of expressing? At the first performance the work started from the eighth bar, and I'm quite happy with this cut. The three solos in the first flute beginning from [C] in the second half were added before my very eyes when I was standing on the conductor's platform after the composer had cut the opening seven bars. In this sense it appears appropriate to cut these opening bars.

I recall that many changes were made for the first performance and that I conducted accordingly.

Papillon

The second flutes establish a tempo suggestive of the tranquillity of autumn which is employed as the basis for the lyrical flight by the first flutes. The mystery, tranquillity and, by extension, dynamism of the natural world are determined here by how the clusters are handled. The key is to strictly observe the instructions of the composer in order to evoke the image of butterflies dancing to a backdrop of a chill, forlorn autumn breeze.

Blue Train
ブルー・トレイン

Tempo I
Allegro moderato

Ryōhei HIROSE

© 1979 by ONGAKU NO TOMO SHA CORP., Tokyo, Japan.

12

Marine City
マリン・シティ

Ryōhei HIROSE

© 1980 by ONGAKU NO TOMO SHA CORP., Tokyo, Japan.

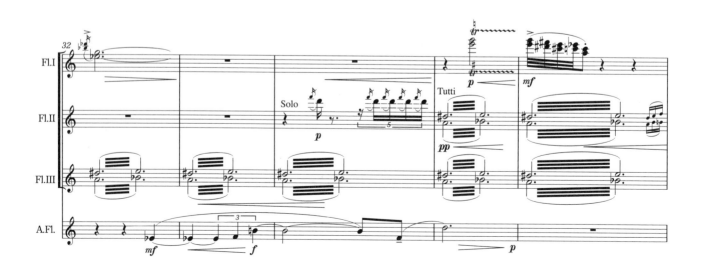

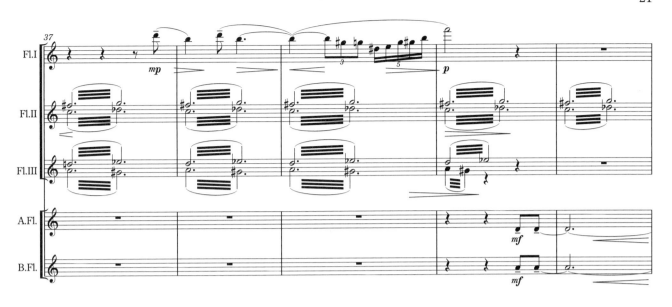
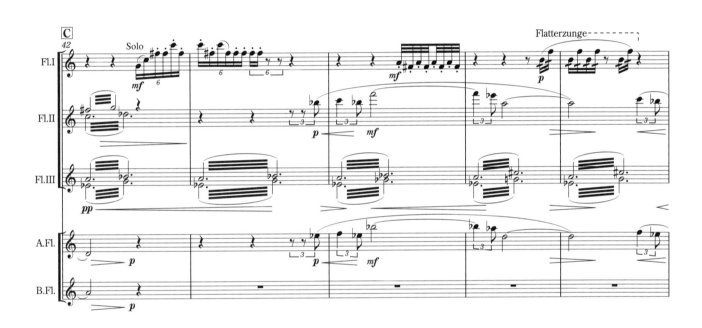
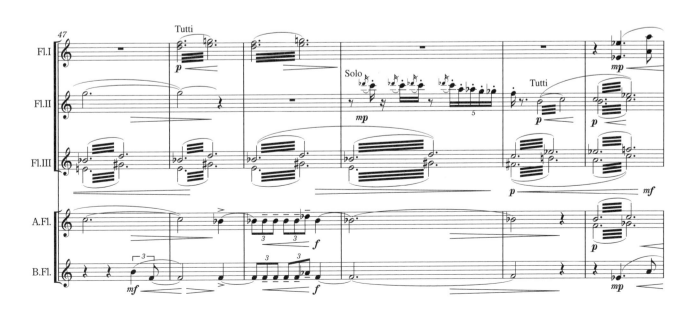

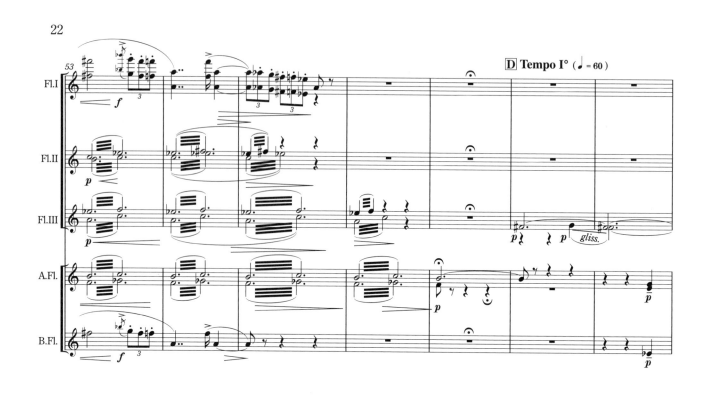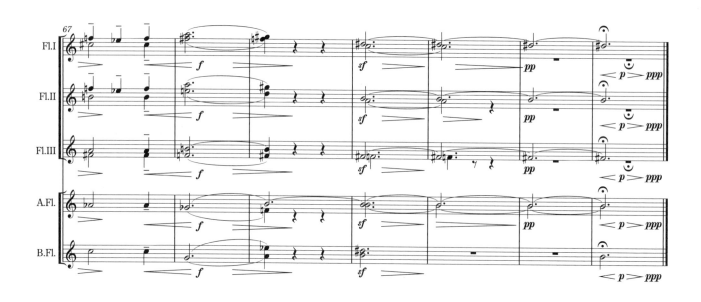

Papillon
パピヨン

Ryōhei HIROSE

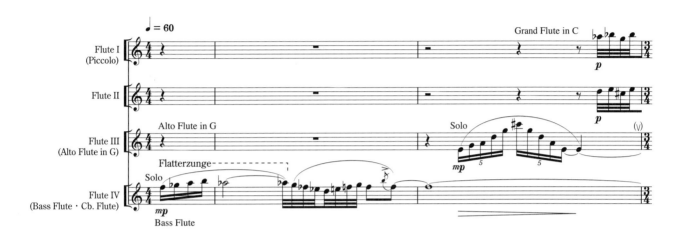
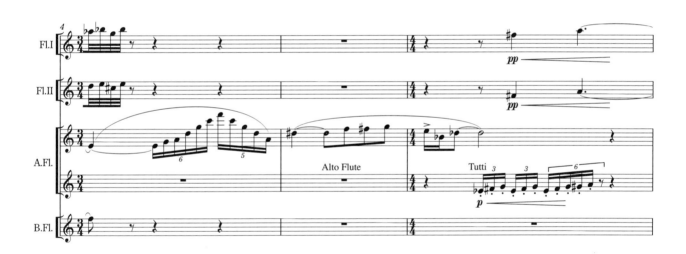

© 1980 by Ryōhei Hirose
© 2018 assigned to ONGAKU NO TOMO SHA CORP., Tokyo, Japan.

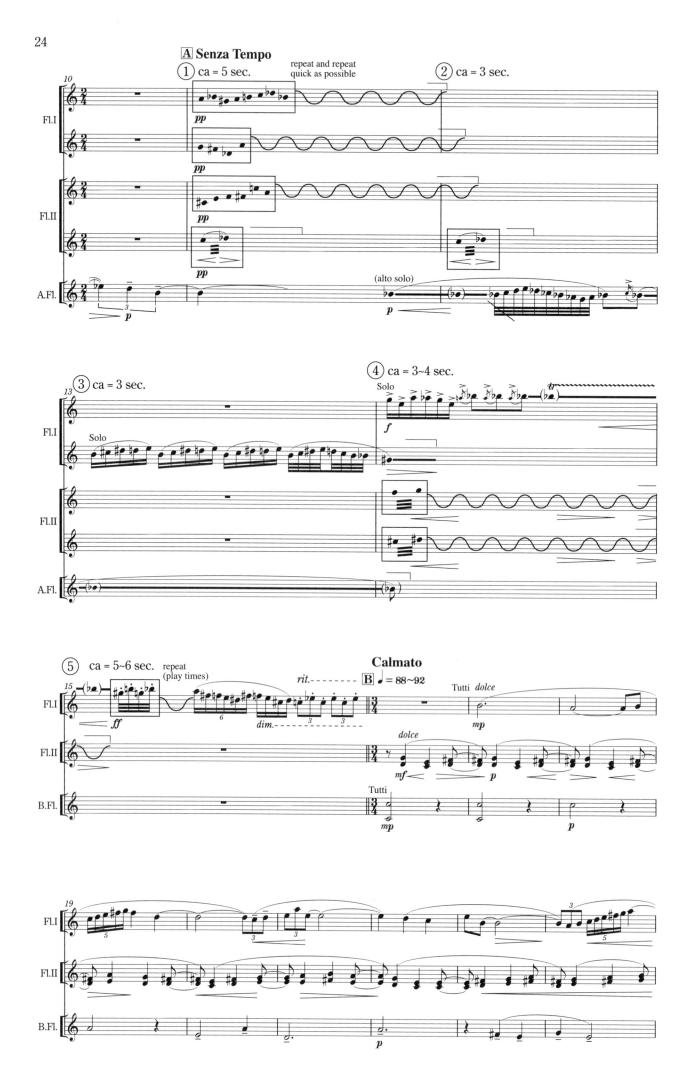

27

廣瀬量平 (1930-2008)

　函館生まれ。生家は市内の老舗レストラン。幼少期から身近に蓄音機があり、ピアノを習うなどクラシック音楽は空気のように身近だった。小学校の後輩は播博。終戦後北海道大学予科に入学、のち新学制の教育学部音楽学科に編入。時の学部長、教育学者の城戸幡太郎に「教育の原点は音楽である」との言葉に背中を押され作曲を志す。と同時期に、後に札幌交響楽団を創設するドイツ帰朝の荒谷正雄が主宰する札幌音楽院に入門し、ドイツ音楽理論を学ぶ。

　北海道大学卒業後に上京、フランス新帰朝の池内友次郎門下に入り、同時に東京藝術大学入学、1963年に同大学院を修了。池内門下でのフランス音楽理論・エクリチュールの修行は非常に厳しいものであったが、後の作曲家生活に全く困らない自信を与えられたという。

　この前後から商業的作曲を始め、スタジオミュージシャンと接するうち、青木明や野口龍（Fl.）等とも邂逅した。次第に委嘱を受けるようになり、最初期の委嘱作《フルートとチェンバロのためのソナタ》（1964）の初演である野口龍は、その後も廣瀬フルート作品の立役者となる。邦楽奏者との出会いも繁く、洋楽技法の熟達者であり洞察者であった廣瀬が邦楽に接することで、尺八に見られるような「息吹」「息づかい」に内なる声や精神性、霊性を見いだし、日本人・日本とは、さらに東洋・西欧とは、という視点から洋楽を見つめ直し、ローカル・グローバルとは、という大きなテーマに踏み出すことになる。これは同様に「息」の楽器、フルートやリコーダーそして尺八作品へと連なり、重要作品群を成した。ことにフルートでは、メロディメーカーであった廣瀬が職人技のように硬軟自在、調性非調性に限らず幅広い作品をつくった。

　フルート関連のコンサートピースは50曲ほど、うちフルート・オーケストラ作品は編曲も含めると30曲を超える。こうした息吹や息づかいから声、歌、精神性、さらには東洋・西欧性への洞察が、廣瀬の三大協奏曲と言われる《尺八協奏曲》（1976）はもちろん、《チェロ協奏曲「悲」》（1971）、《ヴァイオリン協奏曲》（1979）に昇華し、それは合唱曲まで及び、尾高賞ほか芸術祭大賞などの大きな評価を得ることになる。芸術祭優秀賞、芸術作品賞は数知れず、古典化した作品も多い。

　尾高賞を得た1977年より京都市立芸術大学作曲科教授に招聘され、その後音楽学部長。さらに同大伝統音楽研究センターの提唱者にして初代所長。2008年11月24日、京都コンサートホールの館長在職時に没す。78歳。紫綬褒章、旭日小綬章。函館市栄誉賞、京都府文化賞特別功労賞、京都市文化特別功労者賞。

RYŌHEI HIROSE (1930-2008)

Born in Hakodate in a family that were proprietors of one of the city's oldest restaurants, Ryōhei Hirose was raised in an atmosphere pervaded by classical music, with a gramophone and a piano in the home. He studied in the Department of Music in the Faculty of Education at Hokkaido University and began composing with the encouragement of the then head of faculty, Bantarō Kido, who believed that music was the starting point for education. He then began studying German music theory at the Sapporo-Ongaku-in, directed at the time by Masao Araya, who had studied in Germany and was subsequently to create the Sapporo Symphony Orchestra.

Hirose went to Tokyo after graduating from Hokkaido University and began to study with Tomojirō Ikenouchi, who had just returned from France. He also entered the Tokyo National University of Fine Arts and Music, completing his studies in the graduate school in 1963. He underwent an intense course of study of French music theory and style (écriture) under Ikenouchi, and it was this experience that gave him his future self-confidence as a composer.

From around this time he began working as a commercial composer, and his encounters with studio musicians led him to come into contact with the flautists Akira Aoki and Ryū Noguchi. He gradually began to receive commissions, one of the earliest of which was the *Sonata for Flute and Harpsichord* dating from 1964. First performed by Ryū Noguchi, this became the main work in Hirose's output for the flute. Hirose also came into frequent contact with performers of Japanese traditional music. As a musician with insight and mastery of Western musical technique, Hirose, through his contract with traditional music, discovered the inner voice and spirituality that lurks in the breathing techniques employed by the shakuhachi.

He re-examined Western music from a Japanese perspective and taking account of the differences between Asian and European music and began tackling the concepts of 'local' and 'global' in his work. In this light he created a series of important works for instruments for which 'breath' is of the essence, specifically the flute, the recorder and the shakuhachi. As a composer for whom melody was all important, Hirose created a wide range of works, both tonal and atonal, with his characteristic fluency and flexibility.

His total output for the flute includes around fifty concert pieces, of which more than thirty, including arrangements, were scored for flute orchestra. Hirose's insight into breathing techniques, the voice, song, spirituality and the contrast between Asia and Europe came to full fruition in his three most important concertos, *the Concerto for Shakuhachi and Orchestra* (1976), *the Cello Concerto 'Triste'* (1971) and *the Concerto for Violin and Orchestra* (1979) and his works for choir, for which he was awarded numerous prizes including the Otaka Prize and the Grand Prix and other major prizes at the Arts Festival sponsored by the Agency for Cultural Affairs. Many of his works have become classics of their type.

He was appointed professor in the Department of Composition at the Kyoto Municipal University of the Arts in 1977, the year when he was awarded the Otaka Prize, and later became head of the Faculty of Music there. His proposal for creation of a Traditional Music Centre at this university was accepted and he became its first director. Ryōhei Hirose died at the age of 78 on November 24, 2008 while director of the Kyoto Concert Hall. He was the recipient of the Medal with Purple Ribbon, the Order of the Rising Sun, the Prize of Honour of the City of Hakodate, and cultural prizes from the prefecture and city of Kyoto.

青木 明

1956年東京藝術大学音楽学部フルート科卒業。東京フィルハーモニー交響楽団、京都市交響楽団、上野学園大学、武蔵野音楽大学、桐朋学園芸術短期大学、名古屋芸術大学及び大学院教授を経て、現在同大学名誉教授。フルートを故山田忠男、故 吉田雅夫、故 M.モイーズの各氏に師事。現在までに９回のリサイタルを開催する。指揮法を故 渡邉暁雄氏に師事し、東京フルートアンサンブル・アカデミーの創立指揮者としてフルート・オーケストラの創始に尽力する。1961年にツイス木管五重奏団を結成する。日本フルート協会前副会長、日本管打吹奏楽会理事。長年、管打楽器コンクールフルート部門の審査委員長を始め国内外のフルートコンクールの審査員を務め、2016年には日本管打吹奏楽学会よりアカデミー賞（演奏部門）を授与される。

播 博

武蔵野音楽大学卒業後、ABC交響楽団、読売日本交響楽団を経て、ドイツ国立フライブルク音楽大学に留学、オーレル・ニコレに師事する。南西ドイツ放送交響楽団、ビーレフェルト市立歌劇場を経て1974年帰国後、武蔵野音楽大学にて後進の指導にあたる。東京フルートアンサンブル・アカデミーを設立し、ローマ、ミラノ、パリのヨーロッパと、アメリカはシアトル、サンディエゴ、ニューヨークコンベンション、オーストラリアの18都市に及ぶ公演を成功させた。佐々木伸浩、奥 好寛、宇野浩二諸氏に師事。現在、武蔵野音楽大学名誉教授、アジアフルート連盟理事。

山上 友佳子

作曲家、ピアニスト、チェンバリスト。京都市立芸術大学作曲専修卒業。同大学院修了。音楽学部賞受賞。作曲を廣瀬量平、北爪道夫、クリスチャン・マネンに、ピアノを福井尚子に師事。京都国際音楽祭に作曲家、演奏家として参加を皮切りに作編曲活動を始める。廣瀬量平のアシスタントから共作、編曲も多数。京都の秋音楽祭、芸術祭典・京、コンサートホールふくいオープニング事業、「廣瀬量平の世界」（函館市芸術ホール）、「京都文化週間」（於プラハ）等に音楽監督およびピアニストとして出演。同志社女子大学、京都市立芸術大学、京都府立医科大学各講師。廣瀬量平・事務所では廣瀬量平作品のライブラリアン、作品校訂を担当している。

廣瀬周平

廣瀬量平・事務所　制作、代表。
http://www.hiroseryouhei.com

AKIRA AOKI

Akira Aoki studied the flute at the Tokyo National University of Fine Arts and Music, graduating in 1956. He has been a member of the Tokyo Philharmonic Symphony Orchestra and the Kyoto Municipal Symphony Orchestra and has taught at Ueno Gakuen University, Musashino Academia Musicae, Toho Gakuen College of Drama and Music, and the Nagoya University of Arts. He is currently professor emeritus at the Nagoya University of Arts. He studied flute with Tadao Yamada, Masao Yoshida and Marcel Moyse and has given nine solo recitals. He studied conducting under Akio Watanabe and contributed to the establishment of the flute ensemble as the founding conductor of the Tokyo Flute Ensemble Academy. He formed the Twis Wind Quintet in 1961. He serves as deputy chairman of the Japan Flutists Association and director of the Japan Academic Society of Wind Music. For many years he has served as chairman of the board of adjudicators in the flute category of the annual competition organised by the Japan Musical Education and Culture Promotion Society and has served as an adjudicator at many flute competitions inside and outside Japan. He was awarded the Academy Prize in the performance category of the Japan Academic Society of Wind Music in 2016.

HIROSHI HARI

After studying at Musashino Academia Musicae, Hiroshi Hari was active as a member of Japan's ABC Symphony Orchestra and the Yomiuri Nippon Symphony Orchestra. He then travelled to Germany to study the flute under Aurèle Nicolet at the Hochschule für Musik Freiburg. He returned to Japan in 1974 after working with the SWR Symphony Orchestra and the Bielefeld Opera Orchestra and began teaching at his alma mater. He formed the Tokyo Flute Ensemble Academy which, since its establishment, has given successful performances in 18 cities in Europe (Rome, Milan and Paris), the United States (Seattle, San Diego and New York) and Australia. He studied in Japan with Nobuhiro Sasaki, Yoshihiro Oku and Kōji Uno. He is currently professor emeritus at Musashino Academia Musicae and a director of the Asia Flutists Federation.

YUKAKO YAMAGAMI

Composer, pianist and harpsichordist Yukako Yamagami studied in the Department of Composition at the Kyoto Municipal University of Arts, were she was awarded the Music Faculty Prize. She studied composition with Ryōhei Hirose, Michio Kitazume and Christian Manen and piano with Hisako Fukui. She began working as an arranger after making her initial debut as a composer and performer at the Kyoto International Music Festival. She has collaborated with Ryōhei Hirose as both composer and arranger. She has appeared as musical director and pianist at events including the Kyoto Autumn Musical Festival, the Kyō Arts Festival, the events held to mark the opening of Concert Hall Fukui, 'The World of Ryōhei Hirose' at the Hakodate Municipal Arts Hall and the Kyoto Culture Week in Prague. She teaches at Doshisha Women's University, Kyoto Municipal University of Arts, and Kyoto Prefectural University of Medicine. She also serves as librarian and editor of the works of Ryōhei Hirose at the composer's office.

SHŪHEI HIROSE

Ryōhei Hirose's office, Producer.
http://www.hiroseryouhei.com

廣瀬量平の楽譜

〔現代日本の音楽〕
チェロ協奏曲〈悲〉（トリステ） ［オンデマンド版］　　　　　　　　廣瀬量平 作曲
A4・48頁　　　　　　　　　　　　　　　　　　　　　　　　　　　　　ODM-0190

〔現代日本の音楽〕
祝典序曲 ［オンデマンド版］　　　　　　　　　　　　　　　　　　　廣瀬量平 作曲
A4・56頁　　　　　　　　　　　　　　　　　　　　　　　　　　　　　ODM-0191

〔現代日本の音楽〕
打楽器とヴィオラ、チェロのための **コンポジション** ［オンデマンド版］　廣瀬量平 作曲
A4・32頁　　　　　　　　　　　　　　　　　　　　　　　　　　　　　ODM-0192

〔現代日本の音楽〕
フルートのための讃歌 ［オンデマンド版］　　　　　　　　　　　　　廣瀬量平 作曲
A4横・8頁　　　　　　　　　　　　　　　　　　　　　　　　　　　　 ODM-0193

ブラス／吹奏楽のための **祝典音楽** ［オンデマンド版］　　　　　　　　廣瀬量平 作曲
A4・フルスコア48頁＋パート譜　　　　　　　　　　　　　　　　　　　 ODM-1461

皆様へのお願い
　楽譜や歌詞・音楽書などの出版物を権利者に無断で複製（コピー）することは、著作権の侵害（私的利用など特別な場合を除く）にあたり、著作権法により罰せられます。また、出版物からの不法なコピーが行われますと、出版社は正常な出版活動が困難となり、ついには皆様方が必要とされるものも出版できなくなります。
　音楽出版社と日本音楽著作権協会（JASRAC）は、著作者の権利を守り、なおいっそう優れた作品の出版普及に全力をあげて努力してまいります。どうか不法コピーの防止に、皆様方のご協力をお願い申し上げます。
　　　　　　　　　　　　　　　株式会社 音楽之友社
　　　　　　　　　　　　　　　一般社団法人 日本音楽著作権協会

ブルー・トレイン／マリン・シティ／パピヨン
［新版］フルート・オーケストラのための

2019年2月10日　第1刷発行

作曲者　廣瀬量平
校訂者　青木明
　　　　播博
　　　　山上友佳子
発行者　堀内久美雄
　　　　東京都新宿区神楽坂6の30
発行所　株式会社 音楽之友社
　　　　電話 03(3235)2111(代)　〒162-8716
　　　　振替 00170-4-196250
　　　　http://www.ongakunotomo.co.jp/

609044

落丁本・乱丁本はお取替いたします。
Printed in Japan.

楽譜浄書：中村匡寿
翻訳：ロビン・トンプソン
装丁：吉原順一
印刷／製本：(株)平河工業社